Ten Poems
about Dogs

ex libris

Candlestick Press

Published by:
Candlestick Press,
Diversity House, 72 Nottingham Road, Arnold, Nottingham NG5 6LF, UK
https://www.candlestickpress.co.uk/

Design and typesetting by Craig Twigg

Printed by Bayliss Printing Company Ltd of Worksop, UK

Selection © Di Slaney, 2025

Cover illustration © Sam Cannon, 2025
https://samcannonart.co.uk/

Candlestick Press monogram © Barbara Shaw, 2008

© Candlestick Press, 2011 and 2025

First published 2011
Reprinted 2012, 2013, 2014, 2016, 2017, 2018, 2019, 2020, 2022, 2023, 2024 (twice), 2025
Second edition, revised 2025

Donation to Dogs Trust - https://www.dogstrust.org.uk/

ISBN 978 1 913627 70 6

Acknowledgements

The poems in this pamphlet are reprinted from the following books, all by permission of the publishers listed unless stated otherwise. Every effort has been made to trace the copyright holders of the poems published in this book. The editor and publisher apologise if any material has been included without permission, or without the appropriate acknowledgement, and would be glad to be told of anyone who has not been consulted.

Thanks are due to all the copyright holders cited below for their kind permission.

Carole Bromley, poem first published here by kind permission of the author. Jane Burn, *Magma 92* (2025), by kind permission of the author. Jeanette Burton, *Winchester Poetry Prize Anthology* (2022), by kind permission of the author. Billy Collins, *Taking Off Emily Dickinson's Clothes* (Picador, 2000) by kind permission of Chris Calhoun Agency. Jeanne Dubrow, *Stateside: Poems* (Evanston: TriQuarterly Books/Northwestern University Press, 2010) by kind permission of Northwestern University Press. Vince Foxall, poem first published here by kind permission of the author. Caleb Parkin, *This Fruiting Body* (Nine Arches Press, 2021). Siegfried Sassoon, *Collected Poems* (Faber & Faber, 2002) by kind permission of the Barbara Levy Literary Agency. Stevie Smith, *The Collected Poems & Drawings of Stevie Smith* (Faber & Faber; Farar, Strauss & Giroux, 2018).

All permissions cleared courtesy of Dr Suzanne Fairless-Aitken
c/o Swift Permissions swiftpermissions@gmail.com.

Where poets are no longer living, their dates are given.

Contents

Newport

You lead the puppy past the moored boat.
He nuzzles sand, runs to where the waves break,
    snaps at lacquered fish that swim near shore.
You let him off the leash, because you like
    to see the freedom of a loosened thing,
a ball releasing from a hand, a voice
    untying from the collar of the throat.
Each day you walk a little farther, then bring
    him home to me, his tail a muddy spike,
his body soggy as a kitchen mop.
    We don't wring him dry but watch him shake
the ocean out, watch him rub his face across
    the carpet until he falls asleep, sopping,
curled tightly as a seashell on the floor.

Jehane Dubrow

Another Reason Why I Don't Keep a Gun in the House

The neighbors' dog will not stop barking.
He is barking the same high, rhythmic bark
that he barks every time they leave the house.
They must switch him on on their way out.

The neighbors' dog will not stop barking.
I close all the windows in the house
and put on a Beethoven symphony full blast
but I can still hear him muffled under the music,
barking, barking, barking,

and now I can see him sitting in the orchestra,
his head raised confidently as if Beethoven
had included a part for barking dog.

When the record finally ends he is still barking,
sitting there in the oboe section barking,
his eyes fixed on the conductor who is
entreating him with his baton

while the other musicians listen in respectful
silence to the famous barking dog solo,
that endless coda that first established
Beethoven as an innovative genius.

Billy Collins

Doghouse

let the doghair gather
let it clog up vacuum filters
we'll celebrate its drifts
nurture its unruly clumps until
this whole house becomes dog
panting and hapless   it sniffs the crook
of the cul-de-sac like an unwashed crotch
its double-glazed eyes   full of sky
its roof all ears   alert to the breeze
its eaves atwitch   as the dogwood
in our garden leans in   whispers
Squirrel
from each bristling leaf
every tile aquiver

Caleb Parkin

The one thing we underestimate about our dogs

is their ability to show up, unannounced, uninvited,
even if it is just their nose or the tip of their tail,

on every family photograph ever taken. There
you all are, at a summer gathering in the garden,

posing with your margaritas, your sticky BBQ ribs,
the word *cheers* taking shape in everyone's mouths,

when, undetected by even the most astute aunt,
a furry interloper pads nonchalantly into the frame.

You are unlikely to catch your four-legged friend
in the act and though you scroll through images,

sharing countless pics with friends and relatives,
it may take years to discover this photobomber.

And the surprise is akin to that once experienced
by Sir Arthur Conan Doyle on first seeing photos

of the Cottingley Fairies or like those double
exposures where long dead great-grandfathers

ghost the celebrations of great-grandchildren.
But then one day, instead of a funny cat meme,

your sister sends you a tweet of a spaniel playing
the bagpipes. It's a drawing from the Middle Ages

and it sets you thinking about a time before cameras.
Yes, those artists from the past, those medieval

monks who welcomed the patter of paws across
their illustrated manuscripts. Golden hounds chase

pewter rabbits down the margins of some holy text,
a small terrier waits patiently for Christine de Pizan

to finish writing her poem and a nun, embraced
by an initial letter O, holds a puppy to her chest.

And so, returning to your snapshots of parties,
you re-examine the scene with the studied scrutiny

of a scholar holding a candle to his latest masterpiece.
There is your brother with his raised can of beer,

then your mother holding a tray of chicken kebabs,
your kids playing with water pistols on the lawn,

until, finally, there she is, in the corner of the picture,
the flourish of your dog, a miniature illumination.

Jeanette Burton

The Hairy Dog

My dog's so furry I've not seen
His face for years and years;
His eyes are buried out of sight,
I only guess his ears.

When people ask me for his breed,
I do not know or care;
He has the beauty of them all
Hidden beneath his hair.

Herbert Asquith (1881 – 1947)

Corgi

I'm Meg and I'm naughty. Here's what I do;
steal food off the table and eat my own poo,

terrorise cats, chase cars down the street,
chew up the bog brush because it tastes sweet,

lick my own bottom when gran comes to call,
roll in dead birds and burst your new ball,

take a dump on the path that you have to scoop up,
help myself to a slurp from your best china cup,

pick a fight with a dog who's much bigger than me,
attempt to catch pigeons. How hard can it be?

I'm frightened of hoovers, back-packs, the dark,
I run and I hide and I bark and I bark.

What I do like is muck, what I love best are smells
and I just get confused if somebody yells.

I can't understand why you don't feel the same
when I roll in wet cowpats with no sense of shame.

I'll rub it off later on the best sheepskin rug
then jump on your lap for a big, friendly hug.

I know you love me. Oh yes you do!
Just look at my big brown eyes gazing at you.

Carole Bromley

O Pug!

To the Brownes' pug dog, on my lap, in their car, coming home from Norfolk

O Pug, some people do not like you,
But I like you,
Some people say you do not breathe, you snore,
I don't mind,
One person says he is always conscious of your behind,
Is that your fault?

Your own people love you,
All the people in the family that owns you
Love you: Good pug, they cry, Happy pug,
Pug-come-for-a-walk.

You are an old dog now
And in all your life
You have never had cause for a moment's anxiety,
Yet,
In those great eyes of yours,
Those liquid and protuberant orbs,
Lies the shadow of immense insecurity. There
Panic walks.

Yes, yes, I know,
When your mistress is with you,
When your master
Takes you upon his lap,
Just then, for a moment,
Almost you are not frightened.

But at heart you are frightened, you always have been.

O Pug, obstinate old nervous breakdown,
In the midst of *so* much love,
And such comfort,
Still to feel unsafe and be afraid,

How one's heart goes out to you!

Stevie Smith (1902 – 1971)

Man and Dog

Who's this – alone with stone and sky?
It's only my old dog and I –
It's only him; it's only me;
Alone with stone and grass and tree.

What share we most – we two together?
Smells, and awareness of the weather.
What is it makes us more than dust?
My trust in him; in me his trust.

Here's anyhow one decent thing
That life to man and dog can bring;
One decent thing, remultiplied
Till earth's last dog and man have died.

Siegfried Sassoon (1886 – 1967)

Why all dogs are kind

Their eyebrow's evolution was especially for you.
You are their chosen study and they spend
their canine years fathoming your every twitch.

They know the flavour of your mind. You teach them
syllables. They sort them through selective hearing.
You think about moving and their ears go isosceles.

You pick up a lead and learn how action and reaction
result in decibels. You can't walk as fast as they can.
You're an anchor, dragging the fluke of your feet.

They have a city at the base of every sodden post.
Open the door for we do not have a proper notion of thumbs,
the dogs invisibly say. They know everything about you.

They know, most days, that the world is too confusing a place.
They know that you are prone to hiding away. They know
that without them, you probably wouldn't go out.

You wake to find them lapping at your face. This time
in the morning, it's a question of who has the worst-smelling breath.
Their tongues are a hot adoration on your leg.

Their kindness is in the relentless shedding of hair.
Consider the relationship between a dropped biscuit and the floor.
This is the dog's first law of motion.

They moonscape your garden, tally their claws
to your wooden floor. Each night you walk them
under the stars. You palm the soft shell of their heads.

  They
 reap
   the
    air with their tails.

Jane Burn

Dog walking

I walked.
And so the town went
And the countryside came
And there was darkness in the lane.

Then stars, bright, cold, and a feeling of snow.

In the distance
A dog's bark,
Belonging somewhere.

Tired at last,
I dropped under the hedge
So my heat could warm me to sleep.

I woke sequinned with frost
And I shivered and felt the weight of the world I had wasted.
And a dog was there.
One ear missing, a tail bent badly,
Brown eyes shining, seemed to love me madly, terrible breath.

Off we went, walking slowly,
Him with his wonky leg and his wonky hip,
Me with my cowardice to carry.

He steered me home, I don't know how,
I knocked on the door and prayed for forgiveness.

And when there was, we turned to hug him tight
But he had walked off wonkily into the night.

Vince Foxall